SEVEN SATIRES

(1598)

BY

WILLIAM RANKINS

EDITED BY

A. DAVENPORT

UNIVERSITY PRESS OF LIVERPOOL
HODDER & STOUGHTON LTD., LONDON
1948

LIVERPOOL REPRINTS   GENERAL EDITOR

NUMBER 1   L. C. MARTIN

PRINTED IN ENGLAND

EATON PRESS   OVERTON STREET   LIVERPOOL

INTRODUCTION.

I

VERY little is known of William Rankins, the writer of *Seauen Satyres*. The date and place of his birth have not yet been discovered, and the three books that survive of his work tell us nothing of his biography.

His name first appears on the title-page of *A Mirrour of Monsters* (1587) which was 'compiled by Wil. Rankins.' This book (which is in prose) is an attack on stage-plays, but really consists of an account of the marriage of 'Fastus' and 'Luxuria' which is attended by Idleness, Blasphemy and other vices whose characteristics are described. The attack on drama amounts to little more than the repeated assertion, unsupported by detailed evidence, that the vices described are fostered by plays.

In 1588 appeared *The English Ape*, by *W.*R. An epistle signed with the same initials dedicates the book to Sir Christopher Hatton. *The English Ape* (also a prose work) reproaches the English for borrowing all their vices from foreign nations, and discourses on these vices in the moralizing vein of *A Mirrour of Monsters*. The similarity of tone and manner, the style with its trick of looking for alliteration and forcing the phrase to secure it, the lavish and sometimes extraordinary use of brackets for punctuation, and the repetition of favourite ideas and images, make it quite evident that these two books are by the same writer. There are also numerous slight parallels between them and *Seauen Satyres* of 1598. It is not worth while citing these parallels here since they are obvious to anyone who will read the three books in succession.

That the William Rankins of *Seauen Satyres* was the Wil. Rankins and the W.R. of the earlier books can be regarded as certain. It is not demonstrable, although it is highly probable, that the William Rankins of Henslowe's Diary was the same man. Dr. Greg summarizes the information supplied by Henslowe as follows : Rankins, William. (Autograph as above ; otherwise ' Rankens ' ' Rancken(e)s' ' Ranken (e'.) Playwright. Rankins is another of those for whose dramatic career we are entirely dependent on the Diary. He, or some one of his name, had previously written against stage plays. He appears in connection with the Admiral's men only, from whom he received payment for *Mulmutius Dunwallow* as early as 3 Oct. 1598. His subsequent activity is confined to the early months of 1601. Thus we find : *Hannibal and Scipio*, 3, 11, 12 Jan. 1601, with Hathway ; *Skogan and Skelton*, 23, 26 Jan., 5, 8 Feb., 8 Mar. 1601, with the same ; the *Conquest of Spain by John of Gaunt*, 24 Mar., 4, 11, 16 Apr. 1601, with the same. Rankins and Hathway also obtained a small loan from Henslowe, 20/27 Apr. 1601. That in the partnership it was Hathway who dealt with the company would seem likely from a letter from Rowley to Henslowe begging him to ' let mr hathwaye haue his papers againe of the playe of John a gante.' (*Henslowe's Diary*, ed. W. W. Greg, 1908,ii.305.) It does not seem probable that there were two distinct men named William Rankins, one a playwright and the other hostile to plays, both writing in 1598. One might imagine this a possible situation if it were a case of father and son ; but there is not the slightest evidence that it was. In fact we need not hesitate over the inconsistency of Rankins's writing against plays and then becoming a playwright himself ten years later. It is clear that he had a turn for moralizing and that in *A Mirrour of Monsters* he simply took up a popular topic and used it as an excuse for the exercise of his gift. He did the same thing in *The English Ape* and in *Seauen Satyres*. There is no sign that his hostility to the theatre was so rooted as to prevent his making a pound or two by writing plays if the opportunity offered. Even if he genuinely disliked plays in 1587 he may well have changed his mind by 1598. Gosson changed his mind on this subject ; why should not Rankins have changed his? We are probably fairly safe in assuming that there was only one William Rankins.

II

THOUGH *Seauen Satyres* is mentioned by historians of Elizabethan literature, it has not, apparently, been often read. Of those who have read it, Sir Sidney Lee in his account of Rankins in *DNB* and J. P. Collier in his notice (*Bibl. Acc.*, ii. 228) both dismiss Rankins's work as of negligible literary value. This seems unjust. Admittedly, Rankins is a very minor writer, but he has a talent for turning a vivid phrase which occasionally produces a striking line or two such as the following :

> Shees neither vertuous, beawtifull, nor wise,
> And all her grace is but to seeme precise.

> And thou religion draw thy steele bright sword,
> And lop this cursed *Hydra* limbe by limbe,
> Legions of Angels will attend thy word,
> In cristall armor proofe from death and sinne.

> The glasse full brimmed with the sandy hower . . .

> Make a sad doomes day of an infants birth . . .

> Must all the worlds huge sinnes be layd on me?

and the following stanza is well above the average level of Elizabethan verse-making :

How like a King the Marygould doth spred,
The golden circuit of her impald brow,
A whiffing winde that coronet hath shed,
And made her prowde vnknobbed stalke to
    bow,
No longer will the plants her pompe alow.
So haue I seene ere now a goulden Crowne,
In a darke vault his pretious head lay downe.

It must, however, be confessed that it is not
the poetic merit of *Seauen Satyres* that justifies
a reprint, but the interest of the book in other
ways.

Rankins took advantage of the sudden popu-
larity of formal satire which began with the
success of Joseph Hall's *Virgidemiæ*, 1597. In
Satyrus peregrinans, which is a survey of contemporary abuses, garnished in the approved manner
with satirical portrait sketches and Romanized
proper names, he attempts a form of satire
closely related to the Juvenalian kind now
becoming fashionable. He may seem rather old-
fashioned in using stanzas instead of the couplets
which had been, from Lodge's *Fig for Momus*,
the accepted form for Juvenalian satire ; but
stanzas still continued to be used for satire of a
less classical type such as the satirical *Whipper*
poems of 1601. The *Seauen Satyres* themselves
are formal, but not Juvenalian. They are con-
structed on the ingenious idea of exploiting
the connection between the days of the week,
the corresponding astrological planets, the influence of those planets on temperaments, and

the contemporary manifestations of such temperaments. They are therefore a link between such productions of the current satirical spirit as Hall's or Marston's formal Juvenalian satire and Jonson's 'humorous' satire.

The use of the astrological framework entitles *Seauen Satyres* to their small place in the history of literature; and the information they afford about the currency of quite elaborate astrological beliefs makes them an interesting document in the study of the history of ideas. The allusions to contemporary abuses—the raising of rents, 'Machiavellianism,' the tricks of tradesmen, lawyers, usurers and so forth—sometimes throw a little new light on the social conditions of the time, and in other cases are useful as confirming what is already familiar from other sources.

It is a pity that the evidence is not sufficient for us to identify with certainty the '*Artlesse* mome' (p. 9) whose pamphlet Rankins does not approve of. He may be either Nashe or Daniel, but it is impossible to be sure. Similarly, the Atheist (p. 15) may be intended for Marlowe, though again one cannot prove the case. Still, the passages are additional examples of the manner in which literary figures and literary topics were being discussed in London at the height of the Elizabethan age.

One passage is particularly interesting. The story of *Lollus* (p. 26), who was nearly tricked into marrying a boy-actor disguised as a rich heiress, has all the appearance of being a topical story of a practical joke actually carried out, or at least talked about in theatrical circles. If this is so, we may speculate whether Ben Jonson, who was also frequenting theatrical circles in 1598, had heard the story, and whether he carried it in his mind until it flowered into *Epicœne*. Since *Seauen Satyres* deals with 'humorous' types, it is not impossible that Ben Jonson read it. If he did, the character of *Lollus* might have suggested traits for the character of Sir John Daw in *Epicœne*. Collier suggests (loc. cit.) that the *Lollus* anecdote is a 'curious illustration' of the gulling of Slender in *Merry Wives of Windsor*. One might perhaps go a little further and suggest the possibility that the Slender episode had some topicality for the more knowing of contemporary theatre-goers.

Only one copy of *Seauen Satyres* is recorded in the *Short-title Catalogue*. It seemed desirable that the book should be more readily available, and I am grateful to the authorities of the Henry E. Huntington Library for supplying me with photostats of the copy preserved there and for allowing me to use them as the basis of the present text.

Liverpool.   A. DAVENPORT.

Seauen Satyres·

Applyed to the weeke,

including the worlds
ridiculous follyes.

True fælicity described in the Phœnix.

Maulgre.

Whereunto is annexed the wandring Satyre.

By *W. Rankins*, Gent.

Imprinted at London by *Edw. Allde*
for *William Ferbrand :* and are to be sould
at his shop in Lothbury, at the
hither end of Colman
streete. 1 5 9 8.

To his noble minded friend
Iohn Salisbury of *LLewenni,*
Esquire of the body to the
Queenes most excellent
Maiesty.

WHo *bites his lip, when his folly is bitten,*
hath either enuy in his heart, or suspition
in his head: whome I esteeme as the Indians doe
their hedge-bred Serpents, tread on their backs,
and pull out their stings. But of your worthy selfe,
(whose censure vertue will singularly sentence)
I craue an eye cast to these rough cast Satyres,
which are not absurded (though somewhat
rustically mustred) whose neuer forgotten fauours
I fling vp, not downe, in chalenge of all witlesse
vnarmed heedpeeces.

The true affectionate
louer of your vertues.

W. Rankins.

Induction.

OF Loue, of Courtships and of fancies
    force,
Some gilded Braggadochio may discourse :
My shaggy Satyres doe forsake the woods,
Theyr beds of mosse, their vnfrequented
    floodes.
Their Marble cels, their quiet forrest life,   5
To view the manner of this humane strife.
Whose skin is toucht, and will in gall reuert,
My Satyres vow to gall them at the heart.

SATYR. primus
Contra Lunatistam.

FRom woods, to wood and mad conceited   [A4ʳ]
    men,
That with the Moone participate their minde,
I leaue my hollow vast desertfull den,
To tell them the derision of their kinde.
What fond affects what sodaine change I
    finde :   5
How *Proteus*-like, they change their peeuish
    shape,
Yet dare for honors constant guerdon gape.

And are they stable in their lustfull worke,
And still in complet fulnes of desire :
And as the Tortoys in the mud doth lurke,   10
And will not to the labouring streames retyre,
Nor to the bankes of wholsome hearbes   [A4ᵛ]
    aspyre ;
Yet if she see the glimmering of the Sunne,
Contents a while her ougly cell to shun.

So these selfe soothing sots that hide their
    heads   15
In idiotisme and ignoraunces shame,
Their thicke skal'd fins in brightest glory
    spred,
To get the prize when others win the game,
They haue no firmer vertue than a name :
But who so thinkes the signe the substance is,   20
Erres, and his wit doth wander much amisse.

And as the weather so their worth doth
    turne,
Sometime a red, sometime an ashye pale,
Anon like yce, anon like lightenings burne,
Foorthwith foreshewing stormes to euery
    sale,   25
Next night forefiguring a merry gale,
Disposed like the Moone, their mothers
    glory,
The vainest Planet, and most transitory.

And as the serpent shewes her speckled brest,   [A
When as the eye of heauen is in his height,   30
Aduauncing vp her greene inuenom'd crest :
Increasing mallice by the midday light,
And hydes her foule shape in a frosty night.
Soe doe these fickle peasants prate and lye,
Till aduerse darkenes vales prosperity.   35

I seperate the Droane from honny Bees,
I carpe not at the fewer vertuous sort,
I shake the Oke, as well as lower trees :
If Catterpillers taynte it with resort,
I am a Satyre sauage is my sport.   40
So ending heere my immelodious song,
I bid him mend that thinkes he hath the
    wrong.

SATYR. secundus.
Contra Martialistam.

FRom the proude counsell of contrarious   [A5ᵛ]
    winds,
That keep their surly Court on mountaine
    tops,
I roughly come : deceptions to vnbinde,
And scatter in your eyes the vpstart crops
That true borne valor from the Cædar lops :   5
To tell how *Mars* with his stout crew is
    wrong'd,
By apish toyes and what to doults belong'd.

He that can weare a feather all a flaunt,
Speake in the teeth, and make a veriuyce face,
And with a pride his stubble beard but vaunt,   10
As if in him abounded all good grace,
Or were descended from *Ioues* Princely race :   [A6ʳ]
That hath but set his foote on *Callis* sand,
And sweare he fought with *Mounsier* hand
    to hand.

I, and perchaunce in Court hath crackt a kixe,   15
And thinkes he hath *Bellona* at commaund,
And in his bosome beares his amorous
    trickes,
As if loues passion brought him into band,
When loe in Misars plight the wretch doth
    stand :
Loath'd of the wise, not loued of his owne,   20
Yea fooles doe see the foole himselfe in
    moane.

Auerres his courage conquerd Cannas field,
And that his arme can wield great *Neptunes*
　　　mace
Sweares he will make the haughty foe to
　　　yeeld,
And couch like vassailes when they view
　　　his face,　　　　　　　　　　　　　25
What would this Asse doe in a Lyons case?
So looking big cryes out vpon S. *George*,
To tippling goes and fils his eagre gorge.

What is he like but to a sucking childe,　　　[A
Who immitates to speake by elder talke?　　30
But of plaine wordes the youngling is
　　　beguild :
Because he speakes before his feete can
　　　walke,
Yet in *Alcides* buskins will he stalke.
Then first get teeth, speake plain, & learne
　　　the word
And time (perhaps) will teach thee draw a
　　　swoord.　　　　　　　　　　　　　35

And though my browes are Satyre-like
　　　betwist,
With wormwood garland, not with laurel
　　　crowne,
Yet doe I not true Martiallists resist :
Nor can I scandalize their high renowne,
That Bulwarke is too strong to batter downe.　40
But to these stragling humor-pleased mates
I speake, and know that truth the lyar hates.

SATYR. tertius.

Contra Mercurialistam.

Light footed *Fauni* for a while farewell,   [A7ʳ]
　Nimble companions in our Siluane court,
I go where subtiltie and craft do dwell,
Where wise supposed Orators resort,
Where wizards of sweete Art do make a sport.   5
Where golden *Mydas* holds it for his creede,
Apolloes Lute sounds worse than oaten reede.

Behold a Bruite that scarce can hold his pen,
Yet thinks he hath *Caduceus* in his hand,
And that his stile will charme the wisest men,   10
His shipwrack senses will not driue to land,
His ballet-fraughted ship is in a sand :   [A7ᵛ]
And welladay will hardly serue the turne.
Since he is drownd, his Epitaph may burne.

Another *Artelesse* mome bewitcht with
　　praise,   15
Thrusts forth a patched Pamphlet into print,
When fooles on it, as on a pide coat gaze,
His copper words come out of coxecombs
　　mint :
Fluent from Arte, as water from a flint.
Foure bookes he makes foure elbowes to
　　present,   20
By his induction is his bawble meant.

O wretched iudgers of pure golden Arte,
Why do you bribe your wits with leaden
　　　lines?
Vnlawfull censure takes a lawlesse part,
Whilst fondnes deeper wisedome vnder-
　　　mines :　　　　　　　　　　　　　　　25
By this meanes, learnings sacred skill declines.
And yee your selues allowing wrong for
　　　right,
Argue your power to be of lesser might.

These counterfaites are like an *Ebon* tree,　　[A
Whose body beareth neither leafe nor fruite,　30
Nor any sap but cole-black wood to see,
What glory then to that can men impute?
Except all vertuous plants they will refute :
So are these stocks but images of wood,
And barr'd from Art to make their breeding
　　　good.　　　　　　　　　　　　　　　35

But vnto *Hermes* lawfull sonnes in wit,
That scorne the fellowship of seemers so,
I wish them that due honor shall befit,
That they like sweete *Ambrosian* trees may
　　　grow,
Where Science with her compeeres sits arow,　40
But for the race of dolts and all their traine,
I wish them that they haue, headhiding
　　　shame.

SATYR. quartus.
Contra Iouialistam.

WHere the high minded forrest king
     commands,   [A8ᵛ]
And half horst *Centaurs* kemb his dusky locks,
And haue their progres through his spatious
     lands,
Where Vnicornes attend their Lord in flocks,
Whetting their hornes vpon the corall rocks.   5
And when he thirsts do purge the riuers
     brinke,
(For so ought euery mighty Prince to
     drinke.)

Of thence am I : yet enemy to pride
And publique plaguer of the insolent,
I cannot that iniurious ill abide.   10
When mighty men must haue their wisdome
     lent,
And being Landlords buy their wit for rent.   [B1ʳ]
In fine, the fyne he payes will come to light,
And all be forfait to the foole by right.

Let him that cannot guide *Apolloes* seate,   15
Content him with a couch vpon the ground,
Better be silent, though thy place be great,
Than speaking with anothers toong be
     found :
And so betrayd recive a mortall wound,
Which neither peere nor popular redresse,   20
Can cure with all the good thou doest
     possesse.

The Senators of *Rome* would shame to set
And speake but *Placet* like a borrowed word,
Wherein their censures daunced in a net,
Such sacriledge by *Romaines* was abhord,   25
His skull is curst that can no more afford :
But to confirme all doctrine to be good,
Making both one of *Paul* and *Robinhood*.

Behold the climbing ofspring of the Sunne,   [¹
Vnable those fyre-foming steedes to guide,   30
Suffers the Axeltree of heauen to burne,
And to the wrathfull sea doth headlong slide,
Curst by the Signes for his detested pride.
Thus when we thinke our selues begirt with
              blisse,
We practise our owne downefall with a kisse.   35

But yet there are that trace the milke-white
              way,
And follow *Ioue* to his iudiciall seate,
Whose soueraigne wisdome iudgement will
              obey,
From whom doth spring such comfortable
              heat,
That with deep knowledge makes the mind
              repleat.   40
But for those sort, that want of wit doth
              sterue,
Their cap, and common curtsie will not
              serue.

SATYR. quintus.
Contra Venereum.

FRom the sweet field where *Phillis* hangd [B2r]
    hir self,
And Martyr *Dido* dide in sacrifice,
My flesh bepincht with Lar and Fary elfe,
Where *Venus* and hir darling tyrannize
And leane-fac'te louers (more Idolatrize) 5
Where *Lais* ghost in *Lacus dulcis* lies,
Kept downe with false harts that she cannot
    rise.

I stole away: least the prowd *Paphean* queene,
Although my shape be base and ougly ill,
Might send her sonne to haue hir greatnes
    seene, 10
And force insatiat loue against my will :
For her edicts giue life to them that kill, [B2v]
And her sharp lawes are quite exempt from
    reason,
Full of impiety, periury, and treason.

For instance see a seruant wan and pale, 15
Slaue to his mistres beck, her frowne, her
    smile,
An oath commander when his toong doth
    faile :
Whose meacocks heart in agonies doth boile,
And in a world of follies keepes a coile.
And like a Spanniell wayting for a bone, 20
Feedeth his greedy eye with hope alone.

And in that glasse examine but his lines,
How they are peest with *Ouids* excrements,
How he perfumes with roses his rude rimes,
With pearles and rubyes makes her monu-
        ments,   25
Comparing heauen to her habillaments.
When she is worser than a broken glasse,
Which neuer will for any purpose passe.

His lips with thousand kisses courts her   [B
        hand,
And sonnets forth her beawty to the skyes,   30
Where if her comelines be rightly scand,
Shees neither vertuous, beawtifull, nor wise,
And all her grace is but to seeme precise.
Yet doth this woodcock weare himselfe
        away,
By doating on this foule ignoble pray.   35

I honor *Cynthia*, and her nimphlike traine,
That in sweete *Tempe* feast with chastity,
Whose soueraigne beawty coynes doth dis-
        claime,
Knowing prowde eyes shew smallest honesty,
And coulor hath but coulors property.   40
But for the foole that sighes for all he sees,
For his reward I wish him *Vulcanes* fees.

SATYR. sextus.
Contra Saturnistam.

FArewell awhile chill and vnhallowed   [B3^v]
    caues,
Where *Saturne* with deuouring mischiefe
    frets,
Where Melancholly chafes, and madnes raues,
Where pain dead torments torments death
    begets,
Where discontent in ragged habit sits,   5
Where the harsh tunde vnwelcome Screech-
    owle sings,
And buzzing Hornets flye with cobweb
    wings.

For for a while I must associate them,
That reaching Polliticians will be nam'd,
And what is done in countryes far do ken,   10
Vrging that nature all the world hath fram'd,
Affirming God in things is needlesse nam'd :   [B4
But that the influence of the heauen effects
Our good or bad still grac'te by all respects.

That take a pride in damned *Machiauile*,   15
And study his disciples to be thought :
Allowing all deedes be they neu'r so vile.
Such as haue hell-borne *Atheisme* taught,
Accounting scripture customes that are
    naught.
Such as are earnest Turks, where is a Turke,   20
And call the *Alcharon* a godly worke.

Such as are minded with *Pythagoras*,
And hold the transmigration to be true,
That after death mens soules to bruite beasts
       passe,
And then againe transforme their shape anew,   25
That lookt for resurrection is not due.
So liuing in licentious liberty,
Commit foule treasons, rape, and villany.

But oh deere knowledge do not so permit,   [B
Thy reuerent vertues to be scard and
      maym'd :   30
Infuse thy comfort to some sacred wit,
Else will thy holy offerings be disdaind,
And all thy spotlesse excellence be staind.
These Tyrants will disroabe thee of thy right,
And cloth thee with torne garments of
      despight.   35

And thou religion draw thy steele bright
      sword,
And lop this cursed *Hydra* limbe by limbe,
Legions of Angels will attend thy word,
In cristall armor proofe from death and
      sinne :
When thou with triumph shalt the battaile
      winne.   40
And these sold slaues throgh Sathans gate
      shal passe
And liue in boyling leade and burning glasse.

SATYR. septimus.
Contra Sollistam.

THere where the sottish ignoraunt adore,   [B5r]
  The vaine transparant, splendor of the Sun,
Accounting no felicity before,
The rising of his glory be begun,
Yet darke drownde vices will not seeke to
      shun :   5
I was : but now the shade of men I tooke,
Those that the substance of their soule
      forsooke.

Cræsus said wealth was chiefe felicity,
Onely authority deseru'd a throne,
That war for kingdomes was tranquility,   10
And to be honor'd was true heauen alone,
But when by thraldome all this pompe was   [B5v]
      gone :
Solon (quoth he) my soule must needes
      confesse,
In dying well is onely happines.

The sun shines when the Scepter's in the
      hand,   15
The sun shines where the golden Fleece doth
      rest,
Where Ladyes wanton with a carpet band,
(Though it be shut) within the Misers chest,
And where fat Epicures delight to feast :
O golden glory, shall this euer vanish,   20
Where such a God with swaying power doth
      vanquish.

Behold, the morning cheeres the springing
    flower,
The heate of heauen glads the twining vine,
The glasse full brimmed with the sandy
    hower,
These are more glorious than that pride of
    thine,   25
Yet see how sodainely they shall decline :
When like the flower, thy beawty, vine, thy
    wit,
Thy glasse-dust run, and thou in dust shalt
    sit.

How like a King the Marygould doth spred,   [B(
The golden circuit of her impald brow,   30
A whiffing winde that coronet hath shed,
And made her prowde vnknobbed stalke to
    bow,
No longer will the plants her pompe alow.
So haue I seene ere now a goulden Crowne,
In a darke vault his pretious head lay downe. 35

Let him then thinke, that happines will
    thinke,
It lyes not in the glosse of humaine eyes,
How sodainely that vading ioy would
    shrinke,
When euery minute, liuing pleasure dyes,
Like the bright clowded mistnes of the skyes. 40
If wild-bred Satyres so their lesson can,
Tis better be a Satyre than a man.

SPES IMPERFECTA.

[B6v]

THou Treasurer of heauen where hast
    thou clos'd
This hidden wealth of mens true happines?
In nothing humane fancy hath compos'd,
Yet on the earth once dwelt this blessednes,
To bring the earth from cursed wretchednes :   5
Open that secret coffer we may see,
(If not possesse) that heauenly treasury.

SOLA fælicitas.
Christus mihi Phœnix.

IN the balme sweet imparadized wombe,   [B
  Of a choyce Virgin sanctified by grace,
Where second *Adam* had his fleshly home,
Since the first man his glory did deface,
And curse of heauen possest his sinfull race :   5
My Phœnix was with sacred *Manna* bred,
And by the holy Ghost with Angels fed.

Kings of the earth his spicery did make,
Of Franckinsence, pure gold and pleasing
            Mirrh,
A glorious star appeared for his sake,   1
And the melodious cherubins did stir,
And all cælestiall bodyes doth inferre   [B
Chiefe prayse to him : for by his blessed
            birth,
Heauen was well pleas'd, & fruitfull was the
            earth.

My Phœnix, like that swift returning Doue,   15
That in his mouth the branch of Oliue
            brought,
The badge of peace, the ensigne of true loue :
When this base world by sin was suncke to
            naught,
And the earths bosome, was with water
            fraught :
That like the Pellican, pickt from his brest,   20
The bloud that brought his yong ones
            peaceful rest.

That like the rocke, whence liquid cristall
    flowed,
Opened his side to giue the thirstie drinke,
Like the calme winde, that on the red sea
    blowed,
When thankles Israel (weakely) thought to
    sinke,   25
Like the best good the soule of man can
    thinke :
Oh chiefest best, be best, to vs the worst,
Blest be we (by thee blest) the most accurst.

Oh clock me vnderneath thy spreading wing,   [B8r]
Safe sanctuary for a sinfull soule,   30
Where if I sigh, sky-tuned voyces sing,
For thou once pleas'd, nor earth nor ayre
    wil scoule,
Thy feathers shaking stormy winds controule.
The musick of thy note inchaunts huge hell,
Oh let me then within thy shadow dwell.   35

Behold me like a winter-wythered tree,
Or like a Beacon on a barren hill,
Consum'd by sin anothers watch to bee,
Killing to teach another not to kill :
Spoyling my selfe least other wretches spill :   40
Oh sacred bird, a lower pitch vouchsafe,
Touch but my top, and then I shall be safe.

Behold, to saue me from æternall thrall,
My Phœnix takes his flight vnto a crosse,
Not as the faynd *Arabian* bird did fall,   45
Worne out by age, by fire consum'd to
      drosse,
So looseth that which nature makes a losse :   [B8
And of his ashes doth another mount,
Exceeding all faire Foule of rare account.

No no my Phœnix is but yong in yeeres,   50
Immortall too, yet doth he dye for me,
He on the crosse vnto the world appeares,
Offering himselfe on that vnhallowed tree,
To bring my soule to sweet felicity :
But see hearts-ioy my Phœnix liues againe,   55
Passing hell torment with vnspoken paine.

And now he doth ascend his high-built nest,
A place, vnthought, vnknowne, vnseene,
      vnsaid,
Where with omnipotence he shall be blest,
And I behold this sacred Bird obay'd,   60
And I by him there by his merits stayd :
And like a Doue sit by him most content,
Whose innocence makes me so innocent.

SATYRUS PEREGRINANS.

A Bote, a Bote or I shall set my feete,   [C1r]
  Vpon the incke-black bubbles of this
      streame
And with my rough armes these mudde-
      billows greet,
Foule ferry monster waft me to that realme,
Where men in sleepe do wake, & waking
      dreame :   5
Where the feet stands, where ruling heads
      shold be,
And elbowes take the office of the knee.

A shoare, a shoare I long to see the soyle,
(Oh the worlds pleasure of this new-found
      earth,)
They say it will a well staid sence beguile,   10
Bring liberall plenty to a niggard dearth,
Make a sad doomes day of an infants birth :
Now I am heere Ile try conclusions,
Direct degrees, or indirect confusions.

All hayle greene bearded trees, green headed
      men,   15
A high way to a harbour I haue spyde,
Sir where I am, I very faine would ken,   [C1v]
I aske one on a raw boan'd iade doth ride,
And gently treate him deigne to be my
      guide :
The iolly ryder coyly lookes a side,   20
And checks his proude eye least to me it glide.

A hauke my yongster had vpon his fist,
And by his side a fiue groate canuasse bag,
An olde cut suite, with Couentry blew twist,
The collor fac't with oreng-tawny shag,   25
His spurs hung in the belly of his nag :
Vpon his head a Monmouth cap he wore,
With a greene parrats feather broucht before.

He scarce would speake, (for that he said
        he seru'd)
Lollus a gentleman made ploughmans sonne,   30
Who rightly from his birth-right neuer
        swaru'd,
And now in his affaires his horse must run,
For that to wooe, his master had begun ;
I checkt his bit, and would not let him passe,
Till he confest his master was an Asse.   35

And briefly bred him to this short discourse,   [(
I serue (quoth he) a braue imbroadred foole,
Heyre to a sun-shine swayne, yet will
        perforce,
Borrow a tytle from a learned schoole,
(Indeed his grandsire rid vpon a mule)   40
Yet if you will but let me goe my frend,
Ile tell you all his life, but gesse his end.

He is in loue with euery painted face,
Saluting common truls with rybauld lines,
In songs and sonnets taking such a grace,　　45
As if he delu'd for gold in Indian mines,
(But see how fortune such great wit repines)
In this sweet traffique, his bargaines are so
　　　ill,
That he is made a iade by euery Iill.

Heele enter in an *ergo* with the proudest,　　50
And pot a verse with any grammer scholler,
Speake ten at once, his tongue will be the
　　　lowdest,
Take him but downe (O vnexpected dollor)　　[C2ᵛ]
His present passion brings him to a chollor :
With wagers, and with oath at last tis tride,　　55
And then his argument is not denyde.

Take him within the streete, he is a Lord,
And in a Tauerne better than a king,
With thousand brags heele beawtifie the
　　　boord,
But in his purse the beggars bell doth ring,　　60
Yet once a yeere (as Cookoes vse to sing :)
He hath a little stipendary gold,
Which sum, is spent before it can be told.

And once Ile tell you how this gallant sped,
He was inamour'd of a players boy,   65
And certaine sharkers that vpon him fed,
Did soone instruct the stage boy to be coy,
That but with him, he had no other ioy :
In womans queint attyre they drest the lad,
That almost made the foole my maister mad.   70

They soone perswaded him she was an heyre,   [(
And onely daughter to a knight well
        knowne,
He saw her young, rich, amorous and faire,
Haue her he must, or dye he would with
        moane,
In sleepy nights his very soule did groane :   75
Then had not I been stickler in this strife,
The beast had had a male-kinde to his wife.

Heere did I cut this grosse deuice a sunder,
Weary to heare a base absurded tale,
I tooke this foppish babling for a wonder,   80
I kickt his palfrey and began to rayle,
The fellow lookt vpon me very pale :
And spurring of his horse, bad me adew,
And swore (by God) what he had sayd was
        true.

Anon a Muse had brought me vnawares 85
Before a goodly strong built city gate,
I wholy thirsted after those affaires,
And in I entred to behold the state,
All costly thinges were bartred at a rate, [C3v]
Amazd at that I neuer saw before, 90
I heard one sweare an oath, it cost me more.

I start and saw that fellow swore the oath,
Sell that for lesse, than he did sweare it cost,
Thought I, here conscience liues her fullest
growth
Where buyers win by that the seller lost, 95
But yet I durst not be too bould to boast :
For straight I saw *Symonus* in his shop,
A hollow ring of gold with lead drosse stop.

And yet he quickly solde it by the weight :
(Lead was a better friend to him then gold,) 100
I tooke it for a very pretty sleight,
But when the buyer had his money told,
Away he went : and then I might behold,
Simonius rub his arme, and laugh out right,
That hee had done his neighbor wrong for
right. 105

Anon *Lapistus* with his faithlesse fist,
Insceptred with a subtill peece of wood,
Was measuring foorth such trifles as he list,   [C
Hard at his arme his wife my mistres stood,
Commending that, her husband, sold for
          good :   110
Looking the buier wistly in the face,
Whilst Lapist nickt the measure in the space.

Forthwith great *Gurmond* (to his codpeece
          chain'd)
A payre of groate gloues wrapped in his
          hand,
On top of which a nosegay long remaind,   115
Was trudging to lend money vpon land,
Vpon a statute marchant he doth stand :
But gentle sir, take heed you keep your day,
Or els your mortgage shall the forfect pay.

By this time long-gownd *Lumen* walkt
          abroad,   120
Vnder his girdle greene-waxt labels hung,
Although his pace was slow, gold was his
          goad,
And as the Petifogger went, he sung,
His greas'd belt and the waxe together clung:
He sware a mighty oath his writs were
          spoyld,   125
And by that meanes his client should be
          foyld.

I tract his steps, and followed him alloofe,   [C4v]
Weary with those Mecanicke meane deceipts,
At last he entred to a spatious roofe,
Where great men sat in high iudiciall seates,   130
And iuglers play at euen and odde with
      feates :
As (now sir it shall goe with you to day,
To morrow tis against you, you must pay.)

This hall they say is builded of such wood,
That cobwebs on the rafters are not spun,   135
By right the nature of these trees are good,
Yet there beheld I mighty spyders run,
And by their sucking little flyes vndone :
A thing most strange, that poysoned things
      must dwell,
Where nature scarce alloweth them a cell.   140

There stoode *Briarius* with a hundred hands,
And euery one was ready to receiue,
As many sundry toongs, as seas haue sands :
And when he sayd, the truth I do conceiue,
Then meant the hell-hound soonest to   [C5r]
      deceiue.   145
There saw I twelue good fellowes cald
      together,
That would for-sweare their father for a
      feather.

I saw the widdow in a mourning weede,
Wringing her painefull hands to get her right,
Th'oppressed soule tormented with more
      neede,   150
And cruelty with scarlet cloth'd in spight,
As who should say, in bloud is my delight.
Then thought I (ôh there is a Iudge aboue)
Will all this wrong with one true sentence
      moue.

Such sweating for base pelfe, I did behold,   155
Such periuries to get the vpper hand,
The innocent with falshood bought and
      sould,
Such circumstance before the truth was
      scand,
Such scorched conscience markt with
      Sathans brand,
That straight bereft of my Satyrick wit,   160
I was possessed with a frantick fit.

So leauing this vast rumor of mans voyce,   [C
I made my run vnto a riuer side,
Where, sinke or swim, I tooke no better
      choyce,
With desperate leape in, headlong did I glide, 165
And for I would no more repeate this pride,
I did imagine I was in a dreame,
And so concluded my vnorder'd theame.

ASHWEDNESDAY

O Holyest holy three, yet wholy one,   [C6r]
    Vouchsafe the piercing splendor of
        thine eye,
My soules true Martyrdome to looke vpon,
Where thou mayst in-borne penitence espy,
Without the cloke of false hypocrisy :   5
And though my tong proclaimes not publike
        fast,
Yet prayers to prayse thee is my spirits repast.

Behold, to cinders haue I burnt my sinnes,
    An acceptable sacrifice to thee,
Which heauenly ioyes in heauenly mansion
        wins,   10
The ashes on my sad heart scatterd be,
The pensiue patient of all misery :
In my brest mourning sits she like a doue,
And fears through sin to lose sweet Christ
        her loue.

And though I weare no shirt of Cammels   [C6v]
        haire,   15
A boasting shew the flesh to macerate,
Nor lash my body with the whips of care,
Nor on my knocking brest my prayers
        debate,
Nor with high voice my faults deliberate :
Although I strew no ashes on my head,   20
Nor with beguiling abstinence am fed.

Yet see my heart prickt with true faiths
      desire,
With longing to behold thy sacred face,
Whipt with the feare of thy inraged fire,
Which will the pride of all weake brags
      deface,   25
And my soule knocks to haue thy promist
      grace :
With lowly voyce the ashes of my sinnes,
Scatterd abroad : and so my fast begins.

When I do this, I walke not in the streete,
And tell the world my base dissembling
      guile,   30
Nor tread the cold stones with vncouered
      feete,
Such hypocrites their wretched wayes defile :
No let the heart true parts of griefe compile,
That is the sweete Ashwensday I obserue,
Fast still to this, and thou shalt neuer sterue. 35

Lay not my sinnes
O Lord, vnto my
charge.

CAst down those eies dread deere redeem-   [C7ʳ]
      ing Lord,
That shed salt teares for poore *Ierusalem*,
In pitty of my sinnes by thee abhorr'd,
And when thou hast with loue perused them,
By which thou often hast excused men,   5
And seest how headlong I haue run at large,
Yet Lord, lay not my crimes vnto my charge.

Let that sweete toong sayd woman sinne no
      more,
Thy healing hand most kinde Samaritane,
Pronounce a pardon for my hearts deplore,   10
And make my black sinnes whiter than the
      Swan,
Defilde with mischiefes since my life began.
Oh lay not those foule treasons to my charge,   [C7ᵛ]
But stop them, least they run too much at large.

What glory is it that so meane a soule?   15
Earths vassaylage, the wormes subiected slaue,
Whose honor dust downe-trodden doth
      inroule?
Should quite be damnd, whom thy deere
      word may saue,
And thou thy self the purchast praises haue.
Sauiour, I know my sinnes shall haue dis-
      charge,   20
Where mercy with thy merits is so large.

With bloud more pretious than the worlds
    rich wealth,
Remember thou hast ransomd me from hell,
Cald me thine owne, thy sonne, thy sauing
    health,
Prouidedst me a place with thee to dwell,   25
A place which doth all pallaces excell :
Then let me not in deserts run at large,
But take me to thy safe protecting charge.

From foorth thy Temple thou didst banish
    theeues,
That Saints might praise thee where thou   [C
    wast prophand,   30
And creatures liue that on thy name beleeues,
I am thy temple, let it not be staynd,
For there too long hath cursed Sathan raynd.
Cast forth that tempter, giue the feend
    discharge,
Binde that old Serpent least he flye at large.   35

And when I finde that enemy is gone,
That soothes my soule with vile impiety,
Thy name (oh Father) I will call vpon,
And keepe it from bould sinnes society,
And from false pleasures curst variety.   40
Then let thy spirit walke with my spirit at
    large,
And Lord lay not my sinnes vnto my charge.

Who will prayse thee
Lord, within the
Pit.

WIth reuerent toong, and groaning spirit   [C8ᵛ]
    opprest,
My bones like rocks beaten with seas of teares,
And worne with stormy sighs of my vnrest,
Behold *Messias* my vext soule appeares,
Afflicted with a legion of pale feares :   5
And humbly prayes thee Lord to be appeas'd,
That my hearts killing dollor may be easd.

How shall I do thee honor in the graue?
Or praise thee in the darkenes of despaire?
No light of gladnes shines in sorrowes caue,   10
No morning Harp can hymne thy name in care,
Except some comfort to the sence repaire :
Let then one sparke of fauour but appeare,   [D1ʳ]
And I will say my Lord my God is there.

Like withered stubble bended to the ground,   15
The horse, and yoaked Oxe treade on my
    brest,
And ploughmen gash my reynes with many
    a wound
The poisoned adder makes my flesh her nest
(I Lord, and that oppression is my least :)
Yet none but thou canst fling me to the
    graue,   20
O saue me thence and thou shalt worship haue.

Thy seruant *Job* by suffered Sathan tempted,
Knew by thy grace he should be rays'd
    againe,
For, from the pit his body was exempted,
The curst soule-foe, could there no conquest
    gain,   25
Thou gau'st him strength the conflict to
    maintain,
I haue no power, no strength, no force of
    wit,
Then much more Lord preserue me from
    the pit.

Like to a vanquisht bloody battaile won,
Few now are left to beare *Jehouahs* name,   30
Those which escapt from faiths true fight   [D
    have run,
Reserue yet some (though they be halt and
    lame)
For thou canst cure the soule that hath a
    maime.
Let me (sweete Christ) be one thou meanst
    to saue,
Then know I, that I shall not touch the graue.   35

PASSIO CHRISTI.

O Father if it be thy will,
    let this cup passe.

DIuine humane, humane Diuine, (my
    God)
Behold thy sonne, corruptlesse virgins flesh,
Spirit of thee, which with thee hath abod,
Who than thy selfe (of thy selfe) is no lesse,
Vouchsafe thy heauenly issue so to blesse,   5 [D2r]
That, if thou wilt (ô wilt thou without
    wroth)
Let this cup passe I may not taste thereof.

Thy bitter imposition comes of loue,
Therefore thy gracious will, not mine be done,
This bloudy swet a fathers name might
    mooue,   10
But (ô great righteousnes,) what is begun,
Saue many a child, by torment of one sonne :
Father eternall better thine heyre dye,
Than all the rest in vtter darkenes lye.

This anguish like a sucking serpent drawes,   15
My conduit-flowing veines of bloud so fast,
And my sharpe wounding passion will not
    pause,
But shewes me death to come, not torments
    past,
And pale aspect of weakenes stands agast :
Soueraigne of Kings supreme of ioyfull rest,   20
With thy imperiall scepter touch my brest.

But must thy deare begotten smart for all?
Must all the worlds huge sinnes be layd on
    me?
What shall I suffer then? what kinde of thrall?   [D
What cruell bondage? what sharpe misery?   25
What deaths? what frighting horrors must
    there be
If that one sinne and but of one man too,
Deserue hell fire? what shall all mens sinnes
    doe?

For euery sinne of euery seuerall man,
(Sweet Father) must I beare a seuerall hell?   30
Why then my paine is pleasure yet began,
But in the end where must thy chosen dwell?
Where thou wilt Lord I will account all well :
Heauen, hell, death, life, I will endure my
    crosse,
Reckoning for one deaths conquering &
    lifes losse.   35

All plagues, for all, all yoakes, my backe shal
    beare
Which in this brim-full cup of death I put.
And so auoide tempting cold shiuering feare,
For, I will drinke this draught of gall quite
    vp,
And my inuaded spirit from terror shut :   40
So take the resolution of thy Sonne,
For, Father not my will, but thine be done.
           Explicit Christus.

R ESURRECTIO CHRISTI.

ARchangels, Angels, Martyrs, holy Saints,   [D₃ʳ]
  Oh heauens celestiall family appeare,
Giue all your powers vnnaturall restraints,
Sound Cherubin-like musicke in his eare,
(Whose glorious being banisht all hell-feare)   5
The Sonne is ri's, Gods deare elected Sonne,
And now ascends where his first birth begun.

Cloudes clap together with mellodious voice,
And with your softnes cloath his blessed
        brest,
From his great Father heare a thundering
        noyse,   10
That crownes his bright Sonne in eternall
        rest,
Of all (oh onely all) thou art most blest :   [D₃ᵛ]
And earthly men forsake your vaine delight,
Kneele, pray, and praise, this vncompared
        might.

Ionas that in the huge *Leuiathan,*   15
Three hell-darke nights, & dayes imprisoned
        was,
Is like a chosen Prophet come againe,
(Oh how thy word drad king is come to
].   passe?)
So is this Prophet, which doth all surpasse :
Rose from the foggy entrailes of the graue,   20
Mankinde, vngratefull minded-man to saue.

Baptizing *Iohn* that in the wildernes,
]*tes* Liu'd as an exile in that barren land,
Feeding on *Locusts* in his sharp distresse,
]*i.* Subiect to monsters, and at deaths command,   25
 Hath conquer'd all this with his faithfull
  hand
And is returnd : So our Baptizer is,
Who, not with water but with bloud brings
  blisse.

Since whose abode, deuouring hell is frighted,   [ᴵ
Quaking for feare when *Iesus Christ* was
  there,   30
And quick-eyd death become but dimly
  sighted,
And since, when he is nam'd they shake for
  feare,
If but thy name do such amazement beare,
What did the person of so great a king?
Hels victory controule, and kill deaths sting.   35

Then from the fleshly prison of base sinne,
Rise (oh thou foule infected soule of mine)
Arise, or else death will the battaile winne,
And kill thee with a thousand darted crime,
Come quickly from this filthy graue in time,   40
Rise thus, and thou shalt euer rise with ioy,
And as thy Sauiour did thou shalt destroy.

FINIS.

NOTES.

Title-page. *Maulgre.* Maugre, but an odd use of the word, which means ' notwithstanding.' Perhaps with the sense : *The Phœnix* is a pious poem, but, notwithstanding, the ' wandring Satyre ' is annexed to it. Otherwise we must take it as the title of a poem which was not, after all, included in the book. In this case, the word would mean ' displeasure, ill-will, spite.'

Page 3. *John Salisbury.* Born 1567 ; succeeded to the Lleweni estate on the execution in 1586 of his brother, Thomas (for whom see *DNB*) ; Member for Denbigh in the parliament of 43 Elizabeth ; died 1613. See *Complete Baronetage*, ed. G.E.C. (1900), i. 127; Burke, *General Armory* (1878), p. 892; Lewis Dwnn, *Heraldic Visitations* (1846), ii. 330; Pennant, *Tour of Wales* (1784), ii. 28 ; Calendar of the Salisbury Papers, Hist. MSS. Comm., *passim.*

The Indians. Of the West Indies and America. Nashe says of himself and Harvey, ' (with the *Indians*) ... we ... head our inuentions arrowes with Vipers teeth.' Nashe, *Works*, ed. R. B. McKerrow, iii.19.

hedge-bred. The contemptuous meaning (inferior, low-born) is as important as the literal meaning.

Page 5. *Lunatista*. Persons born under the Moon are modest, gentle, patient, placable, apt to be flatterers. Since the Moon is cold and moist, her people are fond of rivers, lakes, etc., and much addicted to fish. See *The Kalendar and Compost of Shepherds*, (c. 1518), ed. G. C. Heseltine (1931) pp. 148-9. They are also very changeable, and subject to great variations of fortune. See Pontanus, *De Rebus Coelestibus*, lib. iv, cap. ' De Luna,' lib. viii, cap. ' De Sole et Luna,' *Opera* (1518), tom. iii, pp. 156 sqq., 227.

Page 6. 39. A favourite image with Rankins. Cf. *A Mirrour of Monsters*, sig. B1ᵛ; *The English Ape*, sig. C3ᵛ.

Page 7. *Martialista*. ' He that is born under Mars in all unhappiness is expert . . . He is full of malice, and ever doing wrongs. Under Mars is born all thieves and robbers that keepeth highways and hurt true men, and night workers, quarrel pickers, boasters and scoffers . . . He is red and angry with black hair and little eyes . . ' *Kalendar of Shepherds*, ed. cit., pp. 143-4.

13. *Callis sand*. The passage must allude to the fighting at Calais in the reign of Mary. Perhaps the capture of Calais by Albert of Austria, and the expedition under Essex which was designed, but not despatched, to retake the

town in 1596 made the old tales of the Calais fighting topical again.

15. *crakt a kixe.* Kex : a hollow, brittle stem such as those of dry fennel. The phrase parodies ' broke a lance.'

Page 8. 22. Apparently the battle of Cannae, 216 B.C ; and ' conquerd ' must therefore be interpreted ' surpassed that shown on.'

Page 9. *Mercurialista.* ' Who so is born under Mercury shall be very subtle of wit, . . . He shall love well to preach and to speak fair rhetoric language, and to talk of philosophy and geometry. He shall love well writing, and to read ever in strange books, . . . And he shall be a gay maker of ballads, songs, metres and rhymes . . . ' *Kalendar of Shepherds,* ed. cit., p. 147.

14. An adaptation of the proverb : he that is born to be hanged will never drown.

15. *Artlesse mome.* This passage may refer to the quarrel about the importance in literary work of ' Art ' (learning and discipline), for which see Nashe, *Wks.* V. 81 sqq., and compare F. A. Yates, *A Study of 'Love's Labour's Lost'* (1936), pp. 73 sqq. Rankins appears to allude to a particular writer, but it is not possible to identify him. Daniel's *First Fowre Bookes of the civile wars* was printed in 1595 ; he was censured for borrowing too much (' patched ' often implied plagiarism or reprehensible borrowing) and for using too many novel double epithets (' copper words '). See *The Returne from Pernassus,*

part 2, I.ii, and Joseph Hall's *Virgidemiæ*, I.vii, VI.i. But the short verse ' arguments ' prefixed to the books of the *Civil Wars* can scarcely, perhaps, be justly described as an ' Induction,' though Rankins certainly uses the word as a title to a short poem (p.4). The Harvey-Nashe quarrel was still going on when Rankins wrote. Nashe professed to write from native talent and experience of life, not from ' Art '; his *Strange Newes* came out in 1592 with the running-title of *Foure Letters Confuted* and divided into sections answering the four letters; he prefixes Epistles which might be described as ' Inductions '; his work is ' patched ' in that passages from Harvey are quoted in italic and then commented on in roman; he was criticized by Harvey for his vocabulary and his plagiarism (Nashe, *Wks.* V. 93 sqq.); and, lastly, he was an Anti-Martinist, and therefore a more likely enemy than Daniel for the Puritan Rankins to attack.

20. *foure elbowes*. An allusion to the professional Fool's costume. Cf. ' I have heard of a fellow would offer to lay a hundred pound wager, that was not worth five bau-bees : and in this kinde you might venter foure of your elbowes : yet God defende your coate shoulde have so many.' *Induction to The Malcontent*, Webster, *Works*, ed. F. L. Lucas, iii. 303.

Page 11. *Iouialista*. Those born under Jupiter are natural rulers. They will seek for glory and honour, love justice and rectitude, and be studious of the public good. See Pontanus, op. cit., lib. viii, cap. 'De Ioue gerituræ domino,' ed. cit., iii. 223b-224. But when the planet is in its least favourable aspect at the nativity, the Jovialist is prodigal and luxurious, superstitious, obstinate, self-conceited and selfish. See Pontanus, ed. cit., iii. 162b-163.

4. *Vnicorne*. For the properties of unicorn horn and the animal's habit of purifying its drinking water by dipping its horn into it, see Nashe, *Wks*. ii. 284. Compare *A Mirrour of Monsters*, sig. F1^r.

11 sqq. The imagery is rather complicated and the thought confused. I interpret: When men of great position borrow their wisdom from others, and, though like landlords possessing land of their own they possess wit of their own, they nevertheless rent the wit of others, paying a 'fine' as a tenant, in the long run the 'fine' will prove insufficient to secure their reputation for wit, which they will forfeit to the true owner, who was a fool all the same for selling his brains in the first place. The allusion is to men who pose as the authors of books they have paid other men to write.

13. *fyne*. Which of the several current meanings is intended is not clear. The word could mean (i) a sum of money paid to the feudal owner on the leasing or transfer of land, (ii) a sum of money paid by the tenant on the commencement of his tenancy to secure his possession although he paid only a small sum or nominal rent, (iii) a

collusive law-suit devised as a means of conveying land.

to light. We may interpret 'too light' since it would do no harm to a tenant if his paying of a 'fine' (i or ii) came to light, whereas an insufficient payment would be unsatisfactory to the landlord and to the literary 'ghost.' The reading 'to light' could be defended: the conveyance by collusive fine could conceivably, in theory, though not in practice, be invalidated if the collusion were brought to the notice of the court; and the cheat would be exposed if it became known that the great man had bought the manuscript he pretended he had written.

15 sqq. For a similar use of the legend of Phaethon and comparable imagery, see *The English Ape*, sig. B2^v.

19. *recive*. The reading of 1598, 'recite,' can be retained only by intolerable wrenching of the sense. If Rankins wrote 'recive' (receive) the printer may have been misled by the context into printing 'recite.'

Page 12 22. sqq. Cf. *A Mirrour of Monsters*, sig. C4^v.

23. *Placet*. Part of the formula of assent when voting for a measure.

24. *daunced in a net*. Could not hide its naked shame. Proverbial. See G. L. Apperson, *English Proverbs and Proverbial Phrases* (1929), s.v. Dance, 9.

28. *Paul and Robinhood*. Tales of Robin Hood was a proverbial phrase for long-winded,

frivolous tales. See Apperson, op. cit., s.v. Robin Hood. I have not noted any other place where St. Paul and Robin Hood are put together, and perhaps the Puritanism of Rankins can be detected in his selecting Paul, the peculiar theologian of the Calvinist, as the greatest contrast to worthless frivolity.

Page 13. *Venereus.* Those born under Venus are amorous, voluptuous, hating evil actions and sordid things, delighting in neatness, delicacy, culture and elegance. But if the dominance of Venus be much shared with Saturn or Mars, the Venerean is dirty-minded, lascivious and unfortunate. See Pontanus, op. cit., lib. viii, cap. 'De Venere cum fuerit genituræ domina,' ed. cit., iii. 225 sqq. If any ' dry ' influence diminishes the pure efficacy of Venus, the Venerean will be effeminate, cowardly, uxorious, spineless and contemptible. (Ibid., 166.)

1. *Phillis.* Daughter of Sitho the Thracian. She fell in love with Demophoon, son of Theseus. When he did not return at the promised time, she died, some say by hanging herself. See Hyginus, *Fabulæ*, 59; Servius, *Ad Ecl.*, v. 10; Ovid, *Heroides*, ii.

2. *Dido.* Cf. *Aeneid*, iv. 584 sqq., vi. 450 sqq ; Ovid, *Heroides*, vii.

5. *And . . . Idolatrize*). If we retain this reading we must interpret : Lovers, who are emaciated for love, idolize their ladies all the more (or, idolize Venus and Cupid all the more) for the

tyranny under which they languish. This is rather strained, and not like Rankins's usual style. A tempting emendation is : ' On leanfac'te louers (mere Idolatries) ' with the meaning : Venus and Cupid, those purely idolatrous objects, tyrannize over lovers.

6. *Lais.* I can give no satisfactory explanation. There were two famous courtesans named Lais. One was buried in the Cornel Grove at Corinth (see Pausanias, II. ii. 4, ed. Frazer, ii. 19, with the editor's note), the other in Thessaly ; and Athenæus describes her tomb thus : ' it is shown by the side of the river Peneus, bearing a stone water-jar . . . ' xiii. 589.b. Whether any garbled version of this lies behind Rankins's statement I cannot say. *Lacus dulcis* should mean ' sweet water lake.'

Page 14. 23. *peest.* Either ' pieced,' i.e. patched out with, or ' peised,' i.e. loaded down with.
excrements. Either beauties which were the ' outgrowth ' of Ovid's genius, or the vile refuse which was the ' lees ' of Ovid's work (referring to the *Ars Amatoria* etc.).

33. *precise.* Puritanical, but usually, as here, with the implication of hypocrisy.

42. *Vulcanes fees.* Alluding to the cuckolding of Vulcan by Venus with Mars.

Page. 15. *Saturnista.* Saturn is generally a malevolent planet, being cold and dry, and hence melancholic. The Saturnine person, born when the moon is in certain aspects, will suffer severely from internal pain, gout, dropsy and anguish of the nerves. With the Moon and Mercury influencing the nativity, the Saturnist is ailing, perverse of mind, utterly corrupt in morals, disloyal and malevolent. With the most favourable aspects, the Saturnist is serious, abstinent, prudent, of good faith and sound judgment, and thus apt to be religious. Hence Rankins's last stanza. See Pontanus, op. cit., lib.viii, cap. 'De Saturno genituræ domino,' ed. cit., iii. 222 sqq.

11. *nature all the world hath fram'd* etc. Cf. *The English Ape*, sig. A3 and Marlowe, *Tamburlaine*, II, vii. 18 sqq. This passage may possibly be aimed at Marlowe. At least it repeats what was reported of Marlowe's opinions. 'Is it pestilent Machiuilian pollicy that thou hast studied? . . . if it be lawfull *Fas & nefas* to doe any thing that is beneficiall, onely Tyrants should possesse the earth . . . The brocher of this Diabolicall Atheisme is dead . . . and wilt thou my friend be his disciple?' Greene, *Groatsworth of Wit* (1592). Marlowe 'denied God' and wrote books affirming 'the holy Bible to be but vaine and idle stories, and all religion but a deuice of pollicie.' Thomas Beard *The Theatre of Gods Judgements* (1597). These and other relevant texts will be found in *The Life of Marlowe*, C. F. Tucker Brooke (1930), pp. 97 sqq.

12. *Affirming God in things is needlesse nam'd.* Affirming materialistic determinism, and denying

any need to suppose the activity or intervention of God in the working of the world.

Page 17. *Sollista.* Those born under the Sun are the natural possessors of high place since under the influence of the Sun are honours, titles and all forms of dominion. Good success and good fortune in the material things of life are also his gift. Gold is especially under the influence of the Sun. See Pontanus, op. cit., lib.iv, cap. ' De Sole,' ed. cit., iii. 155 sqq. Rankins as a Christian and a Puritan rejects this solar type of ' the good life.'

8. *Cræsus.* Cf. ' *Cræssus* whose wealth hath bin woondered at, and whose riches yet remayneth in the mouthes of many. Not giuing eare to be guided by the wysedome of *Solon*, but trusting vnto the vanity of his riches, proudly boasting that, to bee the summe of felicity, was amiddest the ambition of his aboundaunte wealth, taken prysoner by *Cyrus*, when hee confessed no manne to bee happy before his ende, and that vertue consisted not in the aboundaunce of ryches, but in the adorning the mynde with pretious wisedome.' *The English Ape*, sig. B2ᵛ

17. *a carpet band* etc. This is obscure. 'Band' certainly alludes to the bond which the usurer has safely locked up in his chest, but it may also pun on ' bond,' a base fellow. ' Carpet ' is apparently in the usual sense of inactive, boudoir-haunting. Perhaps we should interpret : where ladies flirt with a base fellow who lives in

society only because he has mortgaged his property to a usurer for ready money, and so can shine as a gentleman for a time.

Page 18. 40. *mistnes.* Since this may stand for ' mist'ness ' (mistiness) which gives tolerable sense, it has been retained in the text. It may, however, be a misprint for ' mistres ' i.e. the Moon.

Page 19. *Spes imperfecta.* The allusion is of course to Pandora's box, but the hope is Christ.

Page 20. *Phœnix.* Christ as the Phœnix is a commonplace. See Nashe, *Wks.* ii. 50, iv. 219.

Page 21. 29. *clock.* A possible spelling of ' cloak ' (*OED* records ' clocke '), and therefore retained in the text.

Page 24. 24. *Couentry blew twist.* A thread dyed a special blue colour which was supposed to depend on the water of the river Sherbourne at Coventry. The thread was normally used for embroidery.

25. *oreng-tawny shag.* Cloth having a velvet nap on one side, usually of worsted, but sometimes of silk ; of a dull brownish yellow colour.

27. *Monmouth cap.* A kind of flat cap, much worn by sailors and soldiers. See *Henry V*, IV. vii. 104.

30. *Lollus.* For the name Lollio in connection with gentility upstarting from humble country parentage, see Joseph Hall, *Virgidemiæ* (1598), IV. ii.

Page 24. 40. *rid vpon a mule.* Countrymen rode on mules, but there is clearly some imputation on Lollus' ancestry. There are at least two possibilities. A mule is a hybrid, and the hint may be that the grandsire's wife was the offspring of her rustic mother and a man of rank. Church dignitaries before the reformation rode on mules (see Skelton, ed. Dyce, i.322), and the suggestion may be that Lollus' real grandfather was a churchman, and hence not married to the grandmother.

Page 25. 50. *enter in an ergo.* Ape scholars, who used *ergo* in the university disputations.

51. *pot a verse.* Cap a verse. See quots. in *OED*, pot, *v*¹. III. †7.

60. *beggars bell.* I do not find this as a common proverbial phrase. Perhaps with the notion of the beggar's ringing his empty dish as he begs, and suggested by the proverb : ' A proud mind and a beggar's purse go together.' (*Oxford Bk. of Prov.*, p. 25.)

61. *as Cookoes vse to sing.* I cannot find any proverbial phrase like this, but the cuckoo is proverbial for having only one ' note ' and singing for only a definite and restricted time.

Page 26. 76. *stickler.* Second, supporter.

Page 27. 104. *rub his arme.* A proverbial sign of pleasure. See *Love's Labour's Lost*, V. ii. 109.

Page 28. 109-12. A common jibe. Cf. ' Hee causes his wife to sit in his Ware-house, to no other purpose, then . . . that while his Customers are gaping at her, hee may cosen them of their waight.' Webster, *Wks*. iv.44.

117. *statute marchant*. ' A bond of record, acknowledged before the chief magistrate of a trading town, giving the obligee power of seizure of the land of the obligor if he failed to pay his debt at the appointed time.' *OED*.

119. *forfect*. A possible spelling, and therefore retained, although the word is spelled ' forfait ' on p.11, line 14, above.

121. *greene-waxt labels*. The labels are the strips of parchment inserted at the foot of legal documents to bear the seals. Green wax was used for the seals of *estreats* (certified copies of original court records, especially of fines and amercements) ; and complaints about the green wax were old : Jack Cade demanded that ' all the extorsiners myght be leyd downe, that is to say, ye grene wax the which is falsly used to the perpetuall hurt and distructyon of the trew comyns of Kent.' See *Hist. of the English Bar* (1929), H. Cohen, p.524. The trick here referred to is not clear. Perhaps Lumen pretends that the damage done to the seal from its adhering to the belt invalidates the copy and that a new copy must be procured—and of course a second fee paid to him.

Page 29. 129. *spatious roofe*. Westminster Hall, the usual haunt of lawyers.

131. *feates*. Business transactions.

134. *This hall* etc. Ireland was freed from all venomous creatures by St. Patrick. Irish soil and timber, even when exported, retained the power to drive away venomous creatures. Spiders were, to the Elizabethans, poisonous. 'Westminster Hall built with cobwebless beams conceived of Irish wood.' V. S. Lean, *Collectanea*, ii. 598 sqq., which see for the whole subject.

Page 33. *Lay not my sinnes* etc. An adaptation of the last words of Stephen : ' Lord, lay not this sinne to their charge.' Acts, vii. 60 (Geneva Version).

2. *teares for . . . Ierusalem*. See Matthew, xxiii, xxiv. The phrase is perhaps suggested by Nashe's *Christs Teares over Jerusalem* (1593).

15-19. The printer may be responsible for this unusual punctuation ; but since it is not impossible in Elizabethan usage, it has been retained. A more usual punctuation would be ' soule, . . . inroule, . . . haue?'.

Page 35. *Who will prayse thee* etc. Apparently a conflation of ' in the graue who shall praise thee?' (Psalms, vi.5, Geneva Version) and ' who shall worship thee, O Lord, in the infernall pit?' (Hopkins and Sternhold, Metrical Psalms, 1599 edit.)

Page 37. *O Father* etc. Quoted from memory. ' O my Father, if it be possible, let this cup passe from me . . . ' Matt., xxvi. 39 ; ' Father, If thou wilt, take away this cuppe from me . . . ' Luke, xxii. 42. (Geneva Version.)

Page 37. 12. *Saue.* Query, read ' Saues.'

Page 39. 6. *ri's.* The apostrophe is unusual. Perhaps we should read ' ris ' ' or even ' ris'n.'

18. (——). The Henry E. Huntington Library copy has been cropped, and the marginal notes have been lost. The mark left here could be either a full-stop set rather high, or the end of the arm of an *r* set rather low.

Page 40. 23. (——)*tes.* Possibly the remains of ' *Baptistes* ' or of ' *Locustes.*'

25. (——)*i.* Possibly the remains of ' *Monstri.*'

BIBLIOGRAPHICAL NOTE.

Entered to Ferbrand 3 May, 1598. Arber, *Transcript*, iii. 114.

Title-page: Reproduced on p. 1 above.

Collation: 8º : A-C⁸, D⁴. A2, C4, D4, $ 5-$8 not signed.

Pagination: 1-49 (A4ʳ-D4ʳ).

Running-titles: A3ʳ-A3ᵛ, none; A4ᵛ-B6ʳ, ' *Seauen Satyres* ' (versos) ' *applyed to the weeke.*' (rectos), except for B5ʳ which has, anomalously, ' *Seauen Satyres* '; B6ᵛ, none; B7ʳ-B8ᵛ, ' *Sola fælicitas* ' (versos) ' *Christus mihi Phœnix.*' (rectos); C1ʳ, none; C1ᵛ-C5ᵛ, ' *Satyrus peregrinans.*'; C6ʳ-C6ᵛ, ' *Ashwednesday.*'; C7ʳ, ' *Lay not my sinnes O Lord, &c.*'; C7ᵛ, ' *Lay not my sinnes O Lord* '; C8ʳ, ' *vnto my charge.*'; C8ᵛ, ' *VVho will prayse thee Lord* '; D1ʳ, ' *within the pit.*'; D1ᵛ, ' *VVho will prayse thee Lord, &c.*'; D2ʳ-D2ᵛ, ' *Passio Christi.*'; D3ʳ-D4ʳ, ' *Resurrectio Christi.*'; D4ᵛ, blank.

Contents : A1, missing, presumed blank ; A2ʳ, title-page ; A2ᵛ, blank ; A3ʳ, dedicatory letter to John Salisbury of Lleweni ; A3ᵛ, 'Induction.'; A4ʳ, '*Seauen Satyres applyed* | to the weeke.' (italic and roman) ; B6ᵛ, '*Spes imperfecta.*' ; B7ʳ, 'SOLA fælicitas. | *Christus mihi Phœnix.*' (roman and italic) ; C1ʳ, '*Satyrus* peregrinans.' ; C6ʳ, '*Ashwednesday.*' ; C7ʳ, 'Lay not my sinnes O Lord, vnto my charge.'; C8ᵛ, 'Who will prayse thee Lord, within the Pit.'; D1ᵛ, '*Passio Christi.*' ; D3ʳ, '*Resurrectio Christi.*' ; D4ᵛ, blank.

Notes : Each page of text normally has an upper and lower border of type-ornaments. But when a poem begins at the top of a page, as they all do except *Passio Christi*, the title is within a box of type-ornaments, and the upper border is omitted. Exceptions to this practice are *Induction* and *Spes imperfecta*, of which the titles are printed, without boxes, below the upper border, and *Satyrus peregrinans*, of which the title is printed within the factotum block which also appears on the title-page. The *Seauen Satyres* have second running-titles, printed below the upper border : '*SATYR.1. contra Lunatistam.*', '*SATYR.2. contra Martialistam.*' etc., and *Christus mihi Phœnix* has a similar second running-title on both rectos and versos : '*Christus mihi Phœnix.*'.

The catchword on C1ʳ is 'Or', but the first word on C1ᵛ is 'Sir'. The running-title and the pagination on page 47 (D3ʳ) is in larger type than the rest.

The book was carelessly printed, and the type used was battered. Many letters are broken, but not doubtful. The unique copy has been severely cropped, and the running-titles and pagination numerals have been shaved on many pages. Enough remains, however, to permit the descriptions given above. An early reader has underlined many passages. These have not been noted.

The present Text : The book has not been reprinted page for page, but the signatures are given in the margin opposite the first line of text of the original page. Long f has been abandoned, minute irregularities of spacing have not been preserved or noted, and broken or badly-printing letters have been silently corrected. No changes have been made in the text apart from the following :

PAGE	LINE	PRESENT TEXT	1598	
5	6	change	chãge	
5	15	their	heir	(*But with a space for the* t.)
6	30	height	he ght	

Page	Line	Present Text	1598	
11	5	their	heir	(*But with a space for the* t.)
11	13	will	well	
11	19	recive	recite	
12	40	the	y̆e	(*Black letter.*)
12	42	serue.	sterue.	(*The compositor caught the word from the line above.*)
13	10	seene,	seeme,	
13	16	mistres	misters	
16	41	Sathans	Sathãs	
21	26	thinke :		(*The point is blurred, but looks more like a colon than a full-stop.*)
21	28	thee blest)	thee best)	(*The compositor caught the word from the line above.*)
23	6	stands	stãds	
24	25	fac't	fae't	
28	113	chain'd)	chain'd	
30	159	conscience	cõscience	
		Sathans	Sathãs	
34	27	Then	hen	(*Something got between the type-face and the paper, mutilating the* P *and the* A *above, and obliterating the* T. *An early reader has supplied the letter in MS.*)
34	29	From	Frõ	
34	31	that	ț̆y	(*Black letter.*)
35	17	wound	woūd	
35	18	The	ᴛhe	
36	22	Sathan	sathan	
36	35	that I	that I,	
37	3	thee,	the,	
40	33	beare,	beare?	(*The compositor caught the point of interrogation from the next line.*)